Tails, Scales, Fur, Purr, Oink

Stories and Artwork by Jennifer Foreman de Grassi Williams

Watercolors by Bobbi Kelly

The Williams Family

Volume No 1

Animal Tales of Tails

Affectionately dedicated to my Mother and Sister whose support of my adventures nearly equaled my own exhilaration.

A big THANK YOU to my best friend, Bobbi Kelly, Watercolorist extraordinaire, who has indulged and supported my childhood dream of writing children's books. Bobbi is the artist for several of my other books.

It has been my honor to gently mend countless broken wings, nourish numerous hungry bellies, and offer shelter to a plethora of sentient animals as they journey across my path.

There is certainly an animal heaven!

Contents

Button, Buddy, Bunty and Boo are the four remarkable Williams children who were faced with growing up in a house filled with all assorted animal friends... some cuddly and soft, and others that had big teeth. These sentient creatures taught the four B's many lessons about life, love, caring, sharing, acceptance, sensitivity, perseverance, trust, adventure, dedication, duty, responsibility, empathy, respect, embracing the unusual, and setting something free.

The lessons learned, as hoped by their parents, are that all things deserve to be loved and treated with respect. No doubt the four B's will share childhood

memories with their own children and continue to
be mindful of the footprints they leave in the world,
and never forget that if animals could talk they would
probably speak of all life as being one big family.

The Williams Family Adopts Tiki Turtle

A tale that is mostly true

Story by Jennifer Foreman de Grassi Williams

Watercolors by Bobbi Kelly

Dedicated to my husband who, if he'd had a

crystal ball in 1978, might have decided not to

journey down this road piled high with

fur, feathers, scales, webbed feet, slobber,

fangs, claws and a multitude of 'poop',

literally and figuratively.

The story about Tiki Turtle, who still lives at the Williams house with Pee Wee, is a sweet little rhyme. It is mostly true and partially fiction, about how to care for one of the oldest of souls that lived when dinosaurs roamed the Earth. This story speaks to the caregiving of pet box turtles and how <u>ADOPTION</u> is hard work, sometimes, and a blessing.

If you know about winter and the North wind that howls,

Finding a turtle would make you a hero;

So I'm going to tell you how Tiki was adopted,

The temperature was hovering at just about zero.

Tiki the turtle was forgotten one day,

As she roamed in her yard at the end of the street;

But her new Mom would say she had intelligent eyes,

While hugging, and smiling, and tickling her feet.

"My Mom said she found me all
skinny and cold,

Not fit for hibernation or a long
winter's nap;

So she gave me some food and
nice baths for a drink,

A pink fuzzy sweater, blue
slippers, and her lap!"

Tiki knew being adopted was quite different,

Than some turtles who lived in the deserts and streets;

But life was quite happy and good for the soul,

TV and pillows, heat lamps and sweet treats.

"Are you happy little Tiki?" said Buddy and his sisters,

(sitting close to the fire, and the presents and tree);

"Life is a blessing even more with you in it."

And Tiki just sighed, cuz' "they're talking 'bout me".

Tiki loved eating from a bowl
filled with food,

But the lettuce she ate left her
hungry and sleepy;

What she needed was fruit,
vitamins and protein,

And sometimes a worm as she'd
say, "ugh that's creepy".

Often times, Tiki's 'brother'
would take her outside,

His friends loved to watch Tiki
hide on the ground;

And sometimes, it was scary and
frightening all alone,

Upside down, on her shell, or
completely turned around.

And dangerous too, were the neighborhood dogs,

Who sniffed her and barked with their slobbering jowls;

Luckily, Tiki could tuck in her head,

And soon they accepted her as "one of their pals".

On warm summer days, she
would play with Pee Wee,

And they'd sit by the water
that was needed for drinking;

It got pretty warm and then
hotter from the sun,

"Mother where are you?
I'm too hot, and
I'm shrinking!"

Because temperatures can start
to get dangerously high,

Tiki's friend, Pee Wee, jumped
in the water to cool;

Feeling kind of nervous Tiki knew
Pee Wee couldn't swim,

So threw out a life saver to the
side of the pool.

"Mother can't always be there to watch me,

As I venture in places she knows aren't the safest;

Like the time a raccoon bit off parts of my toes,

And the doctor had to stitch them in places."

"And though I'm adopted my family wouldn't trade me,

And certainly my needs can be somewhat a bother;

Especially because I can live to be ninety,

But they love me , my siblings, my mother and father."

The End

Pet Box Turtle Facts:

1. Pet box turtles should not be outside in the winter, or any temperature below 50 degrees. They should have shelter from the hot sun of the day (up to 95 degrees in the warmest spot).

2. Pet box turtles need to have a shaded area and a sunny area to hide from or bask in the sunshine.

3. Pet box turtles should not be hibernated if skinny and weak.

4. Pet box turtles need water for drinking and soaking, but not too deep as they don't swim very well. Recommended water depth should be 1.5-2 times the width of the turtle, allowing them to swim a little, but also right themselves if they flip over.

5. Pet box turtles can accidentally flip over and should always be upright.

6. Pet box turtles can drown if the water is too deep. And if the unfortunate happens, like a turtle flipping over and drowning in a shallow pond, there is nothing to stop you from giving it mouth to beak CPR. This happened and is true.

7. Pet box turtles cannot survive on lettuce alone. They need vegetables, fruit, protein, minerals and vitamins (occasionally).

8. Pet box turtles should be protected from dogs, foxes, raccoons, and other animals that might think they are a tasty morsel.

9. Pet box turtles need lots of room. Outdoor enclosures are preferable, depending on year-round weather. Aquariums or small storage tubs are simply not big enough. A rectangular box, approximately 3' wide x 6'long x 1.5' tall, is best.

10. Pet box turtles may need their beaks and toenails trimmed.

11. Pet box turtles are known to live as long as humans if properly cared for.

12. Pet box turtles can get sick, so watch for any signs that a turtle is not feeling well, and seek medical attention. Have a veterinarian check turtles for parasites.

13. Pet box turtles with red eyes are generally male, while females may have brown or yellow. The bottom of a male turtle's shell is usually concave.

14. Pet box turtles can lay eggs. If a fresh one is found, there are a variety of ways to hatch them. However, some eggs are laid when turtles are stressed and may not hatch.

15. Pet box turtles will become friendlier and more responsive if held and talked to on a regular basis.

16. Pet box turtles should be handled, but you should always wash your hands with soap and water after doing so.

Adopting an animal that is wounded, homeless, or just needs a home is one of the greatest gifts we can give.

In the words of Gandhi:

"A society will be judged according to how they treat animals."

Pee Wee and Tiki

A Very Special Thank You to Dr. Alicia Konsella DVM

who speaks with animals daily and gave her sage advice

on the facts in this story.

The Williams Family and a Very Beloved Dolly

When you know a favorite toy has a soul

Story and Artwork by
Jennifer Foreman de Grassi Williams

Dedicated to all toys and the children who have loved them, my Mother who loved her Emy doll and taught me to love dolls, and my first grandchild, Norah Alings 'Cheeky Monkey', who without a doubt will cherish the one toy that she believes is real.

Story number 2 is about a very beloved cloth dolly that was made by a very dear, creative, and loving friend of the author. The dolly was given to Bunty, the middle child, in 1982. In 1985 the dolly was given to Bunty's newborn sister, Boo. This is a story, in rhyme, about Dolly's journey in the family and how she was so loved that the author told her daughter, Boo, that she would run into a burning house to save Dolly. This is a story about human love that is given unconditionally and thoughtfully to a favorite toy in which a soul was born.

The box at the door was a happy surprise,

As it held something precious, but what could it be?

So I'll tell you this story 'bout a gift from the heart,

For a 'cheeky' baby girl, with the pet name "Bunty".

Made by the hands of a loving,
dear friend,

Sewing each stitch with the
patience of few;

An apron, a button, some red yarn
for hair,

A present so special with a secret
no one knew.

It would take 30 years for this secret to unfold,

For this gift made with love was like love of a mother;

And passed from dear Bunty to her little sis Boo,

Beginning the adventure with new sisters and a brother.

Boo loved this dolly and at night they would snuggle,

Telling stories they'd rock and even giggle with joy;

Guarded by bear or tucked into her shirt,

Boo and her dolly, her very favorite toy.

Dolly had hair that was red as a crayon,

That Boo for security would stick up her nose;

That made her brother and sisters laugh harder,

But why she did it only Boo knows.

Adventures were many as the duo
went through life,

With bamboo and a safety pin they
caught a Redfish trout;

Together at the zoo to watch the
monkeys play,

Even in a hospital when Boo had
her appendix out!

Sharing sweet treats at a tea party
with Gramsie,

Crying when Button stole her, or
the time her arm came off;

Riding in a wagon, on a big wheels,
or a trike,

Being Boo's companion when she
had a sore throat or a cough.

Dolly's big adventure was to ride high in the sky,

In a hot air balloon all over the place;

At Christmas she'd sit by the stockings with care,

And wait for dear Santa to come down the fireplace.

Sweet Boo had grown up and graduated too,

Even went to college so very far away;

And Boo took Dolly to live the college life,

Rode the elevator in the dorm, and kneeled at her bed to pray.

Holding Gramsie's hand on the day
she went to heaven,

And even after Boo got married
Dolly moved out too;

When Dolly started losing hair and
features on her face,

Mommy knew that when you're
loved there's something
you must do.

In a baby blanket warm, Boo's
mommy would send Dolly,

To the lady who had made her
nearly 30 years before;

Another dolly was created with
everything brand new,

And Dolly crawled inside to be
the heart and soul and more.

The lesson and the secret too, for children and their friends,

Who have a dolly or a bear, a bunny, or a troll;

Love remains when you get old or ragged 'round the edges,

And touches your heart because you know you gave your toy a soul.

The End

To take Dolly out of her new body

- Separate hair and unzip

- Take out Dolly's head first

- Lift out her arms and then her torso

- Lift out legs

- Give Dolly a warm hug

To put Dolly into her new body

- Hug Dolly

- Put padded cap on Dolly's head

- Place Dolly's head face down into her new head

- Fold up Dolly's feet and fit into legs. It might feel like trying to put a snowsuit on a one year old. You have to help Dolly push her legs in and pulling her new legs up

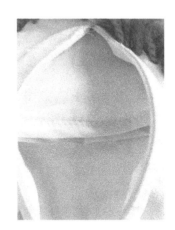

- Ease her torso in

- Fold Dolly's hands up and place arms along the sides of her back

- Tuck her in "snug as a bug"

- Lift up as you zip closed

Scattered Spools
Michell Nietfeld's One-of-a-kind
hand made items
http://scatteredspools.wordpress.
com/home/about-4/blog/

The Dolly Project

Michell Nietfeld and Scattered Spools

Creativity and design are my passions. I fill my days creating one-of-a-kind clothing for children and adults, handbags and a variety of other fabric products. I find extreme joy in creating items for people from loved ones clothing. Any "retired" clothing can be used creatively to find new life.

A Very Special Thank You to Michell for lovingly

creating Dolly nearly three decades ago and believing

that Dolly really does have a soul.

The Williams Family Bids Aloha to Shell and Lily

When you love something enough to set it free

Story by Jennifer Foreman de Grassi Williams

Watercolors by Bobbi Kelly

Dedicated to
my wonderful mother who,
like Shell and Lily,
was a very wise and old soul.

Story number 3 is about two Africa Spur-thighed Sulcata tortoises, Shell and Lily. They were rescued as young tortoises, and came to live at the Williams house where they were loved by everyone. They had very curious habits, like pushing open doors, sitting by the smaller box turtles that lived in their yard, resting on indoor heater vents to stay warm, burrowing into their bedding, loving to be hand fed, exploring the neighborhood (unaccompanied), and bumping into you to get your attention. As they continued to grow, it was obvious that they would need bigger accommodations and a warmer climate. It was a tough decision, but a right decision, to find an environment that would give them more freedom, sunshine most of the year, and more choices for a natural diet. The old adage about letting something you love be free has many lessons, and so the journey for Shell and Lily to the Makauwahi Cave Reserve on the Island of Kaua'i became the perfect solution. And fortunately, the Williams family can volunteer at the Reserve and visit their beloved tortoises.

It happened one day that a tortoise named Shell,

Came to an art room to visit the class;

He lived in a small tub, but then he just grew;

He needed more room and a field of grass.

His family loved having him inside
the house,

But, he'd have to wear a diaper as
he just didn't know,

That the fruit and the grasses,
the vegetables and leaves,

Sometimes made Shell have to
potty, PRONTO!

The neighborhood kids liked to feed and pet Shell,

But he was so lonely and even quite blue;

So a new tortoise came to live at his home,

Shell was so happy, and tortoise Lily was too.

In winter when Shell had to sleep in the house,

Lily would sleep in a shed on her bed;

Shell thought he'd show off and ate Christmas lights;

They just about killed him, the green,
yellow, and red.

Summertime in Idaho
was lazy and warm,

So down the back hill they
escaped to explore;

A mail truck rescued them from
the wildlife and creek,

The foxes and ospreys, speeding
cars and much more.

Lily and Shell loved their family and friends,

But needed more sun and more room just to roam;

Tortoises, like them, lived on Earth since dinosaurs,

But where was a place that could be a better home?

A long flight would take them to
the land of the sun,

With white sandy beaches instead
of the snow;

Kaua'i would be home with her
chickens and ocean,

Makauwahi Cave was the place
that they'd go.

Shell and Lily wore shirts that were funny,

While stomping and eating the very bad weeds;

The plants that were native could grow and be pretty,

And they'd live to 100 while doing good deeds.

The Cave with its limestone had
fossils and shells,

And around it was farmland for
tortoises to graze;

And so they would live on this
beautiful island,

Restore native plants, their
purpose most days.

Because they could burrow when it's hot, or too cold,

Kaua'i was so perfect for these herbivores;

The challenge would be what to eat or not bother,

Or to eat just as much as a noisy lawn mower.

They spent days exploring and made some new friends,

These friends could say baa baa and even quack quack;

What a sight to behold all these animals together,

Wool, shells, and feathers just covered their backs.

Lily and Shell will be missed by their family,

But the gift they deserve is one we call freedom;

Look for them surfing or high in the sky,

Aloha sweet tortoises, your lives are so awesome!

The End

Pet Sulcata (African Spurred) Tortoise Facts:

1. Pet Sulcata's are originally from the African continent, and live to be over 100 years old (something to consider).

2. Pet Sulcata's begin life at about 2" long, but grow to about 36" and can weigh 200 pounds as an adult. Growth rates vary a lot, and generally females are smaller. The Sulcata is the third largest tortoise in the world.

3. Pet Sulcata's must be kept in dry, hot environments. They burrow to escape high temperatures (above 80 degrees) and must avoid cold and damp temperatures. Cool nights, rainy weather and winter (below 50 degrees) must find these 'gentle giants' indoors. A UVB light is important so they can process calcium in their diets. All lights should be turned off at night. A warm garage is ideal.

4. Pet Sulcata's are herbivores and eat vegetables, herbaceous plants and grasses, leaves (mulberry, grape, hibiscus, hollyhock) and flowers, especially roses. No pesticides please! Orchard grass and Timothy hay are great for larger tortoises. A spring mix of lettuce, kale, turnip and collard greens is good. Cactus pads add variety and the Mazuri Tortoise Diet is a great supplement. How they love to graze, especially in grass and shrub lands.

5. Pet Sulcata's need powdered calcium and multivitamin supplements.

6. Pet Sulcata's can present challenges to their owners as they outgrow their habitats, get stronger, wander, and need a proper diet and protection from colder climates.

7. Pet Sulcata's have been the subject of an ongoing debate about buying wild animals. You should never buy a Sulcata that is less than 4" long. The Sulcata is not a protected species, while some tortoises are.

8. Pet Sulcata's should have access to an outdoor area that has plenty of grasses for grazing, with enclosure walls of at least 24" in height, as well as the same below ground to discourage their habit of digging. However, they also need a place to escape extreme weather.

9. Pet Sulcata's require some humidity, like that afforded by a natural burrow. This keeps them from dehydrating and maintains smooth shells, not lumpy, as they grow.

10. Pet Sulcata's need an absorbant and natural substrate like Timothy or Bermuda hay, alfalfa, orchard grass, etc.

11. Pet Sulcata's need a water source for drinking and soaking. Using a low sided bowl or creating a mud puddle is a good idea. Some tortoises go weeks without drinking, but long dry spells require that they stay hydrated.

12. Pet Sulcata's can get sick if they do not have a proper diet, or they may suffer from respiratory infections, especially if they get cold or stay wet. Sometimes a cough indicates they are sick.

13. Pet Sulcata's, especially babies, can get stressed if over-handled. Care needs to be taken for their safety. Always wash your hands with soap and water after doing so.

14. Pet Sulcata's, if brought up with love, nurturing and respect become very friendly and will respond to your voice and follow you around.

*These animals lived during the time of dinosaurs millions of years ago, so imagine if they could talk!

*Information about the Makauwahi Cave Reserve can be found at http://www.cavereserve.org/

*"Can Unwanted Suburban Tortoises Rescue Native Hawaiian Plants?" The Tortoise, Volume 1 ~ Number 1, publication of the Turtle Conservancy

A Very Special Thank you to the thousands of staff (Linz, Billie, Joe) and supporters at the Makauwahi Cave Reserve and the work they continue to do to restore and conserve the native species of flora and fauna at the Cave Reserve, and especially many kudos to Managers Lida Pigott Burney and Dr. David Burney for their continued efforts with weed control by using, in part, these amazing tortoises, and encouraging Shell and Lily's journey. Thank you to Dr. Alicia Konsella DVM who consulted with the author regarding the facts in this book about Sulcata tortoises and gave her blessing for their safe passage to Kaua'i.

*When Shell and Lily were young, it was thought that they were both females. As adults, the truth is they are both males!

The Williams Family and Andy Cat

When the loss of a pet really, really hurts

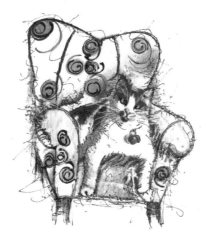

Story and Artwork
by
Jennifer Foreman de Grassi Williams

Dedicated to felines worldwide, both feral
and those lucky enough to have a home, and
the wonderful people who have taken the time
to appreciate these most amazing, and quite
misunderstood sentient creatures.

To:
Andy, Spooky, Jitters, Julius, Groucho, Bun-
Bun, Katina, Swee-Pea, Pooh Bear, Mama Kitty,
Sunshine, Thumper-Willy, Jello, Freddy, Olive,
Raisin, Oliver, Muffy, Goofus, Tubbs, Bear,
Timmy, Ghost, Stickers, Inky, Weezer, Chewy,
Monkey, Toby, Rascal, Hermy, Riley, Callie,
Tommy-Boca, Tia, Zucchini,Tigger, Phantom,
Boo, Tony, Moo, Molly, Spirit, Boots, Buddy,
Charlie, Sammy, Louie, Danny Boone, Boo-boo

Story number 4 is about two cats, but mostly Andy cat, who found their way to the Williams house years ago. Each was a stray that just showed up. The question of where they came from or who they belonged to, initially, was never answered. Andy came first and found himself having to share the house with a number of other cat friends and a surfeit of animals that lived in the Williams menagerie. When Spooky came on the scene it took several years for him to trust the Williams family, until he started shadowing Andy cat everywhere, and saw that Andy liked the Williams'. The day Spooky followed Andy right into the house, we knew he had been initiated into our family. Sometimes it was difficult to allow the five felines that lived with us to roam freely through the neighborhood and down the back hill to the creek where all kinds of raccoons, foxes, and birds of prey journeyed. But this is the autonomy that cats require, as they are free spirits to their core and seek adventure in everything they do. There were few incidents that made us worry about the hours that the cats were out exploring, until the evening Spooky disappeared (forever), and then Andy cat three weeks later. Untold hours of walking, driving, and searching desperately finally yielded only a few clues as to the disappearance of these precious cats. A coyote in the area was the suspected culprit. Searching is one thing. Reconciling the facts is another.

Remembering is forever. All animals are special in their own right, but those that become our pets are rarely forgotten. And those that make their way into the center of our hearts leave a terrible void when they cross the Rainbow Bridge. Andy Cat was such a guy. To think of Andy Cat is a mix of painful longing to hold and kiss him, and also a joy in knowing that we were lucky enough to have had him in our lives.

Andy

Spooky

Andy had a silly face with eyes so crossed and blue,

And Mom would say that everyday his face she kissed and kissed;

Good thing she wore no lipstick, or his face would be quite red,

Oh quirky, funny Andy cat you'll be forever missed.

Andy cat would crouch, then run,
whenever he could hear,

The sound of tape as it unwound
from near his catnip mouse;

He'd try to eat it as it stuck to his
sweet lips and fur,

Oh silly cat we'd laugh and watch
as he'd run through the house.

Andy's very best, best friend in all
of the cat world,

Followed him from room to room
and everywhere outside;

Sweet Spooky lived to sleep and
play and be by Andy's side,

And how sweet Andy missed him
when dear Spooky kitty died.

Another one of Andy's pals would sit on the front porch,

Together they would watch for mice, then come into the house;

Andy followed Tommy up the stairs to watch the birds,

And wondered why on Tommy's fur was stuck a tiny mouse.

WilliAMs

Dear Andy cat loved hunting snakes along the winding creek,

And how he'd sprint up through the weeds whenever we would call;

And stand beside the birdbath, where his tongue just reached the water,

Looking like a big giraffe with neck and legs so tall.

Loveable and loyal, our great big
Andy cat,

Oh how he liked to sleep on
pillows, beds, and in the hall;

And even on our driveway when
the sun just got too warm,

You'd find him sound asleep next
to a pot and fabric doll.

Of course there were the times when our Andy cat would watch,

As Daisy dog would tease and play, first run and then just walk;

And Shelly tortoise grazed on flowers, grass and big old weeds,

The three of them like old, old friends though none of them could talk.

Andy made us laugh and cry
whenever he would hide,

As we could always see his eyes so
crossed and very blue;

He really thought that he could
catch the squirrels in our yard,

But 'round his neck we hung a bell
to warn the critters too.

Crazy, funny, silly cat we think of all the things,

Like when you'd kick a blanket with your bouncy rabbit feet;

And then another favorite thing that you would like to do,

Was bite Mom's hair, no matter where, 'cuz she thought it was sweet.

And even Norah 'Cheeky Monkey'
knew what "kitty" meant,

When Jitters, Spooky, Andy too
would sleep right next to her;

She'd squeal with delight and try
to hold onto a tail,

And all of them liked being there
and said it with a 'purr'.

One night when all the stars were out our Andy cat did go,

It was to be the last of nights with Andy on the ridge;

But we're convinced he sits atop a very special place,

With Grandma, Spooky and his pals across the Rainbow Bridge.

The End

Cat Facts:

1. Cats have unique personalities, which can vary greatly. Some cats are shy/timid, while others are highly social, outgoing, and independent. It may take a period of weeks (sometimes even months) for a cat to adjust to its new home and family. Be sure you are willing to give your new cat some time to adjust. Two cats are sometimes better than one, especially if they are left alone a lot.

2. Cats can live 15-20 years. Be sure you are willing to take responsibility for your new cat for the duration of his/her lifetime.

3. Cats require consistent medical care. Annually (at least), they require an exam to assess and maintain good health and should be kept up to date on vaccinations and de-worming. Be prepared for unexpected medical emergencies, and understand that the cost can be hundreds or thousands of

dollars. Spaying or Neutering a cat as soon as possible makes for a happier cat, plus helping with the cat overpopulation problem facing our nation.

4. Cats, like humans and dogs, develop dental disease and may need dental cleanings and/or tooth extractions. Besides their teeth, a cat's coat can tell a lot about their health, hydration, and whether or not they have fleas, ticks, dry skin, an abscess or sore.

5. Cats, like humans, need to be considered when brought into a new home. Are there other pets? Does your current pet get along with other animals? Are you aware of anyone in the home that is allergic to Cats? Researchers are beginning to find that owning a cat can actually have health benefits like: decreasing the chance of allergies, having a calming effect that could also lower your blood pressure, reduce stress, and help with depression and loneliness.

6. Cats may require a specific diet to manage health issues. Be sure you are willing and able to follow dietary recommendations if this is indicated for your cat. Try to accommodate a picky eater with food that is healthy.

7. Cats require routine care provided by their human family members. Food and fresh water should be provided daily. Look for age appropriate food, and understand that cats, like humans, are what they eat (except in the case of those wild 'things' they eat!). The litter box should be scooped at least once daily. Grooming and nail trimming may need to be performed at home, by a groomer, or veterinarian.

8. Cats absolutely need to be engaged in routine play, especially if they are indoor cats. This helps to keep them stimulated, prevents boredom, and also provides other health benefits. Don't be surprised to find a complete roll of toilet paper unwound, tape chewed and clawed, flower arrangements in pieces,

and holiday ornaments broken and strewn around your house (or a cat half-way up your tree).

9. Cats, both indoor and out, require "resources" to maintain a healthy living environment. These might include: a variety of toys, scratching posts/substrates, bedding, perches, resting areas, outdoor shelter, and adequate litter box(es). Cats delight in string, plastic, bags, boxes, catnip anything, feathers, balls, and bells. It is not uncommon for them to chase their tails, or jump around for a 'phantom' toy. They will play on their own, with each other, or with their owners. Prepare to be snubbed, or made to feel like a fool. If they don't want to play, they won't. It is not uncommon for a cat to walk across your piano or computer keyboard, jump onto a counter or table during a meal.

10. Cat (or pet) insurance is good if you can afford it. Cats are prone to all kinds of mishaps like getting caught in a garage door, getting shut in a dryer, cat fights, tails caught, falling from high places, falling

into pools and ponds, climbing too high in a tree, or getting hit by a car.

Some cats can be very aloof, like Andy cat. It is like going to the zoo when the monkeys look at your antics, and then just walk away. Get used to being ignored by your cat.

You may wonder what cats really think about you. Do they like you or not? Are they just tolerating you? Are they in the mood for your attention? Are they somehow judging your every move?
If cats could talk, they wouldn't. But if they could, they'd say, "What can you do for me?"

Some cats are very verbal and might meow until they are fed. They may choose to bury food in a rug like it's something that belongs in a cat box.

Cats will walk in on intimate moments and just sit and stare. Get used to it.

Always expect the unexpected. Some cats have been known to back up against you and spray, and usually because you have made them mad. They can be unpredictable, as they are purring one moment and turning on you the next.

Cats like to make muffins (not the food kind) on you by moving their paws in a kneading motion. Sometimes this action is soft and soothing, and sometimes it involves their claws on your bare skin.

Cats, if very independent, might take off for a day or two. It is a good idea to microchip your cat and to have a collar with an identifying tag around the neck. If you have a cat that delights in chasing small critters, then hang a large bell too. All cats in our neighborhood wear bells. It kind of sounds like Christmas.

*Please, please spay and neuter your cats!

A Heartfelt thank you to Dr. Robin Roller DMV at the Boise Cat Clinic, and her loving staff, for understanding the unique and special nature of our feline friends. Thank you, too, for consulting with the author regarding the facts in this story about cats, and for being there more than once when tears were shed.

Thank you to the many, many people (both friend and stranger) who helped with the relentless search for Andy Cat and Spooky.

Thank you to the quirky and unique cats that have warmed the author's home since she was a little girl, and who have brought immeasurable joy and laughter with their antics.

Thank you to Andy Cat, who was the King of them all. May your walk beyond the Rainbow Bridge find you showing everyone the red kisses that cover your adorable face.

The Williams Family and a Curious Stinky Minky

When animals teach us the importance of having fun and being curious

Story by Jennifer Foreman de Grassi Williams

Watercolors by Bobbi Kelly

Dedicated to~

Hilly, Ty, Jess, and Em who so loved Minky~

Jak-Jak and Wankar who created their own level
of ferret mischief~

All the people who have taken these amazing
'trouble-makers' into their homes ~ You only
think you owned them!

And as always, to my precocious little
granddaughter, Norah, and her soon-to-be
cousin, baby Clements, who will have to carry
forward our love and appreciation for the world
of animals great and small~

Story number 5 is yet another 'tail', about a ferret who was loved and treasured. He created great angst among our children, sometimes, when they had to share him. Time limits or drawing straws had to be effected for fairness in holding him, and occasionally a child would stomp away in frustration.

Bringing a ferret into the house can throw daily routines out the window. A peaceful environment can change in a minute, and anything lying on the floor is fair game for a ferret to steal. A pile of 'stolen' ferret goods is about as 'strangely unbelievable' as discovering what is under your 5-year-old's bed.

From out of nowhere, Minky would attack your ankles or toes as you passed by a bed or couch. If he was missing, you'd have to check the heater vents, clothes dryer (as he'd bury himself in piles of clothes and fall asleep), dishwasher, or you might see him run by the sliding glass door, because somehow he squeezed through a screen onto a back deck. He was the first thing we'd all look for when returning home, and the last thing we'd look for before going to bed.

After only one week of ownership, we realized that he was not going to be a caged pet, because he was the ultimate escape artist. He was smart and loyal, knew when to play rough or gentle, and trusted to be held and bent into shapes that resembled large pretzels.

Though de-scented, you could always tell if it was your shirt he had been lying on, or your pillow. Somehow you got used to his little skunk-like odor. He dragged more things around that he 'found', and some even twice his size and weight. His favorite of all toys was his little yellow Woodstock birdie.

One day when he became a little old man... having lived a life of fun, danger, and love... he waited until all of us arrived home from school. He consumed the entirety of the family circle we made and took his last breath as we all said our goodbyes. For a very long time our house became oddly quiet, and it took a long time before any of us could walk by a bed or couch and not expect him just to jump out and attack your toes.

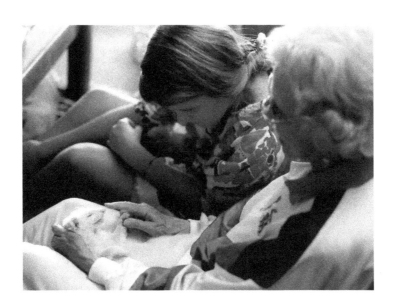

The kids started giggling as they
stared in the window,

As the curious fluff ball was really
a hoot;

Was he a squirrel or maybe a rat?

And his red eyes just made him so
very darn cute!

It was love at first sight as he melted our hearts,

Our daughter adored him more than Dorothy loved Toto;

To show her affection for dear little Minky,

She posed for senior pictures with him in the photo.

Minky, the ferret, made us laugh with his antics,

Stealing and hiding some things that could squirm;

Q-tips, red socks, leather gloves in a pile,

Toys under beds, plus a fat mealworm.

The kids played a game they called 'just find the Mink',

Escape was his talent when he'd slide down a vent;

And then reappear underneath our back deck,

Or asleep in the shape of a pretzel all bent.

At Christmas you'd find him way
up in the tree,

Underneath all the branches to
jump at your toes;

Or scaring the cat when he leaped
from above,

Even licking your lips, and inside
of your nose.

Minky had nicknames like Bogus and Hoffie,

As silly as the tunnels he made in the snow;

He'd climb, hide and get lost 'cuz that's what he did,

Jumping and showing off, plus things we won't know.

Exploring outside Mink would turn turtles over,

His curious nature found him always exploring;

Luckily he stayed 'round the house and backyard,

His life was so fun and never, never boring.

Minky ate things that weren't good for his belly,

Like grapes, and some crackers and even a bee;

And creepy, and crawly, and wiggly too,

But his favorites were spiders that hung in a tree.

Mink's favorite toy was a birdie called Woodstock,

Together they'd hunt for balloons they could pop;

He'd add everything to the piles he kept,

And this made him happy and for that he'd hop, HOP!

Minky would hide, but your nose
could still find him,

'Cuz his odor was kind of a little
bit skunky;

Your bed, or my bed, he'd pick by
himself,

Silly little Mink with his hair funky
and punky!

He taught us to play and to be
very curious,

And waited 'til we all could be
there to say 'bye';

Surrounding him with love, and
the love that he gave us,

Not one of us could talk, or have
a dry eye.

The End

Pet Ferret Facts:

1. Ferrets are the clowns of the animal world. They are extremely high-energy, curious, entertaining, spontaneous, funny, and will need more supervision than most dogs or cats. While a huge responsibility, they will be one of the most unique and fun-loving of all pets if given ample attention, love, and training.

2. Ferrets can live 6 to 10 years if cared for properly.

3. Ferrets require consistent medical care, including regular vaccinations and veterinary checkups, as they are susceptible to heart worms and canine distemper.

4. Ferrets should be neutered before the age of six months for a healthier and happier existence. As a female remains in heat for long periods of time if not mated, a hormone that is produced can make the ferret sick and even cause death. Male ferrets that are

neutered are less likely to display aggressive behaviors and a 'musky' odor that is produced when a male is in heat.

5. Ferrets are very clean animals by nature and will lick and groom themselves like a cat. They will even wash their faces, so should always have access to a water source for that, and for drinking. If desired, a monthly bath for your ferret is good, but use baby shampoo and lukewarm water, followed by a baby or organic conditioner. Frequent bedding changes help reduce odor, too.

6. Ferrets have scent glands near their anus, and like skunks, they can release secretions when startled or scared. However, the smell is much less potent and dissipates more rapidly. Most pet ferrets in the United States are sold de-scented.

7. Ferrets keep everyone on their toes. Be sure to

be prepared for the unexpected medical emergency as ferrets might squeeze down heater/dryer vents, climb inside of a recliner, dishwasher or dryer, or get stuck under a porch. Trying to completely ferret-proof a house is challenging.

8. Ferrets can wiggle and squeeze through nearly anything. It might be a good idea to have a well-ventilated and clean cage that a ferret has access to and can be put in for safety when nobody is around. However, caging a ferret all the time would be like kenneling a cat all the time. Teaching a ferret to be part of the family is the most fun of all and makes for a healthier pet.

9. Ferret cages, if used at all, should be equipped with several levels. The bottom level should have newspaper or a litter box, with upper levels having sleeping hammocks and strong food bowls that cannot be moved or tipped. Litter should be paper-based, and even

shredded paper is good. Pelleted litters work great, too. Avoid clay as it is too dusty and will get up their noses when digging in it.

10. Ferrets will pick up anything they can carry to 'ferret away'. Don't be surprised if your ferret steals gloves, socks, underwear, bags, balloons, pens, toys, etc. and nearly anything else they perceive to be theirs. They will usually create several piles around the house; under furniture, beds and in corners. Be careful that they don't have access to exposed cords and wires, things that break, poisonous substances, or soft rubbery items that they might chew and swallow and get stuck in their guts. They are curious about everything.

11. Ferrets do not do well in extreme temperatures, though they tolerate cooler temperatures better than hot. Anything above 80 degrees should be avoided.

12. Ferrets are a member of the weasel family and are very smart. They can be trained, quite easily, to use a litter box, though they need access immediately when they need to 'go'. Because a ferret's digestive tract is not very long, they can't just 'hold it' like a cat or dog. They may choose several corners of a room if they cannot make it to their litter box in time.

13. Ferret adoption is a family decision for consideration. Do you have any other pets? Does your current pet get along with other animals? Are you aware of anyone in the home that might be allergic? Because ferrets are very social, it is even recommended that they be adopted in pairs for socialization and companionship.

14. Ferrets do like to chase and may even 'nip' at your ankles or feet. Ferrets can be trained not to do this, as their little teeth are very sharp. Telling them 'no' in an affirmative way will usually do the trick. Ferrets

LOVE to play and will even taunt you like a cat, or chase you. They will play-fight and even arch their backs and jump from side to side to engage you in play. Play right back with them and even run away when they chase you. They will love it!

15. Ferrets require routine care provided by their human family members. Food and fresh water should be provided daily. The litter box should be cleaned regularly. As ferrets are from the weasel family, and not rodents, they have very high metabolisms and need meat and animal fats in their diets. There are great ferret foods on the market, but read the labels as some contain fish. Ferrets do not eat fish. They can be picky eaters, so experiment with small quantities at first. Do not feed ferrets canned cat or dog food, carbohydrates, milk (as they are lactose intolerant), fruit or veggies (except as a treat only once and awhile), chocolate, breads or grains, and no grapes.

16. Ferret ownership may not be legal in all states, so be certain to check for any restrictions.

17. Ferrets are not the appropriate pet for some family situations, so give thoughtful consideration if thinking of adopting from a pet store, or a pet rescue. Consulting with a veterinarian is the best of all resources for questions about ferrets.

*Ferrets sleep an average of 18-20 hours a day

*Ferrets are the third most popular pet in the United States

*The word "ferret" comes from the Latin 'furonem', which means 'thief'

*Male ferrets are 'Hobs'

*Neutered male ferrets are 'Gibs'

*Vasectomized males are 'Hob lets'

*Female ferrets are 'Jills'

*Spayed females are 'Sprites'

*Ferrets less than one year old are called 'Kits'

*A family group of ferrets is a 'Business'

*When ferrets get really excited, they may present a behavior called the 'weasel war dance', in which a frenzied series of sideways hops, leaps, and bumping into nearby objects occurs. This is not an aggressive behavior, but is their happy way of saying "let's play". It can be done in conjunction with a soft clucking noise called 'dooking'. If scared or upset, ferrets might make a hissing noise, or a soft 'squeaking' noise.

Sometimes saying "Thank you" seems a bit trite, especially when a person has helped your family so many times. Dr. Alicia Konsella DVM, at the Intermountain Pet Hospital, has continually been a kind and compassionate sounding board for our family and the surplus of questions our family always seems to have about the plethora of creatures we bring into our homes. And if the truth were known, she might just admit that ferrets are her very favorite little beasties!

The Williams Family Rescues a Piggy Named Otis

A moral about finding beauty under many layers

Story and Artwork by
Jennifer Foreman de Grassi Williams

Dedicated to~
My Mother whose love for pigs was very
contagious,
and my three piggly wiggly granddaughters whom
I adore:
Norah Alings, Sonja Hope, and Harper Mae

Story number 6 is a testimony to not judging something by its exterior. Otis came to us by accident when a friend mentioned that a sweet potbellied pig baby was forced to live in a small area between two buildings in her apartment complex. The young piggy never saw the light of day, and was forced to live in filthy conditions, on old towels and blankets, that were stacked and never changed. The owners gave permission for Otis to be removed and taken to the Williams home to be adopted, which turned out to be a birthday surprise for Emily who loved him at first sight. It is certainly amazing the wide range of

comments as people responded to
this curious little piggy being walked
through the neighborhood on a
leash. Time proved that Otis would
test many situations, outsmarting
us more times than not. He was
resourceful, clever, intelligent,
ingenious, and quite resilient in never giving up on

trying something over and over
again. It was also surprising to
me how strangers would comment
that he wasn't very pretty, when I

thought he was stunning! It seemed unfair to judge him so quickly. And indubitably as the years passed, the adage 'beauty is only skin deep' would not apply to him at all. He continually revealed himself to be a complicated and multifaceted, sentient being. Each layer of his self, from complex calculations for great escapes, to the steadfast loyalty he showed to his family, would confirm just how beautiful he was, <u>layer by layer</u>, and to his very core.

The sweetest, cutest little piggy
looked into my eyes,

And grunted once, but that was all,
because he was afraid;

Between two buildings he was raised,
without the warm, warm sun,

But when I smiled and he snorted, a
friend for life we made.

Otis was a muddy mess, and really
smelly too,

But Mommy didn't really care and
put him in her car;

A birthday gift is what he'd be for
Em a great surprise,

And though his coat was really black
his forehead had a star.

It was no secret that dear Em and
Gramsie loved all pigs,

The three of them together was a
happy thing to see;

Otis with his big red leash was cute
as any bug,

He'd prance and snort as they would
walk around a big old tree.

Hilly liked to feed him as he'd eat
most anything,

Potato peels and dessert and any
table scraps;

He'd gobble all the food that she
would put into his mouth,

And never once was bothered by
two very curious cats.

One day when it was pet day at their tiny little school,

Sweet Otis got to ride the bus and sit up in the front;

Oh how the children laughed and screamed to see a pig at school,

But all that little Otis did was wag his tail and grunt.

Otis loved to root around the turtles
in the yard,

He liked to snort into the weeds and
get a rub from Jess;

Inside his house filled up with straw
his little bed was clean,

But put him near some mud and dirt
and he'd be quite the mess.

Pigs are smart as smart can be and
Otis proved he was,

As he'd unlock most any gate with
only his wet snout;

Escape he would into the yard, or
even down the street,

His 'piggies' carrying him away
because he'd gotten out.

WILLIAMS

Another thing that Otis liked almost
as much as food,

Were any blankets he could find on
beds or in a pile;

He'd root in them and try to hide
when Ty would call his name,

But all you'd see was one big nose,
and one big Otis smile!

Carried in a shirt or jacket when he was so small,

Made anyone who saw his snout exclaim "IS THAT A PIG?"

And as he grew he loved the sun and wanted to be scratched,

Behind his ears, or on his belly that grew and grew so big.

One day our very sweet old pig got
sick and couldn't move,

Off to the vet to get him checked
from head down to his toes;

And so we had to get some help to
lift him in a truck,

And there he sat right next to Mom
with a wet and runny nose.

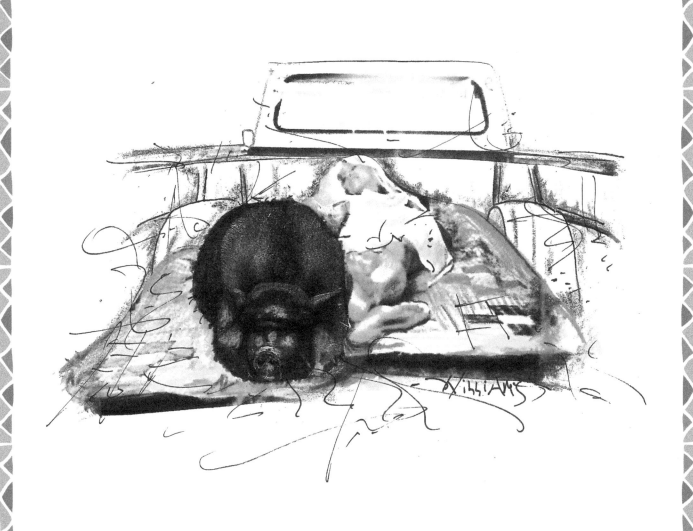

As he grew and got so old his sweet old face would wrinkle,

And certainly his Santa belly got so round and big;

But if we had a choice or chance to do it one more time,

We'd surely choose to share our lives with such a loving pig.

The End

Potbellied Pig Facts:

1. Potbellied pigs are related to other types of pigs, including those farmed, and also wild boars.

2. Potbellied pigs love to bask in the sunshine. And while most of them are black, which affords a little bit of natural buffer from getting sun burned, shade must be provided.

3. Potbellied pigs are innately clean. However, in the wild, they will wallow in the mud, which then protects their skin. There are important nutrients in the dirt and grass that they need as well.

4. Potbellied pigs cannot see very well. And as they get older, their faces tend to scrunch like a folded piece of material, and sometimes they can't see anything. Don't be fooled, however, as their other senses are very keen, especially if food is near.

5. Potbellied pigs are one of the most sociable

creatures alive. They would gladly curl up on your lap, even when they reach maturity between 3-5 years, and weigh 80-160 pounds! They love and crave attention, and will roll over to have their bellies rubbed.

6.   Potbellied pigs are very smart. They can be house trained to use a litter box, or potty outdoors. They can be taught tricks, and even do things like opening cabinets, latches, lifting gates, etc. by observing somebody else doing it, or if they receive a reward. While it isn't necessary for them to do tricks, it is important that they be taught manners and commands like "sit" or "shake" (a hand). Never underestimate their innate intelligence, or how something needs to be their idea to do.

7.   Potbellied pigs do not like to be carried or hugged, except when young, like you would do with a dog. It is through their snouts that they show affection. They love to nudge everything (probably a carryover from nursing when young). Their noses can be tender, and mostly wet.

8.   Potbellied pigs need vaccinations, and should absolutely be neutered by a qualified veterinarian who understands these unique animals. Pigs can get ill, but lack of hydration and obesity are two of the biggest health threats.

9.   Potbellied pigs will eat anything, even bacon I dare say. They are inexpensive to feed, but should be given a healthy diet of low calorie vegetables, fiber, and grain (not cat or dog chow, or canned veggies) twice daily, plus outdoor grazing is vital to good health. They should also have constant access to fresh water for drinking, and a kiddie pool to enjoy.

10. Potbellied pigs can be leash trained and taken on walks. However, they can be stubborn and might need to be coaxed and rewarded with treats. They can even be trained to sit in a car!

11. Potbellied pigs can live to be 12-15 years old, but only if they do not become obese, are allowed social interaction (which keeps them emotionally

happy), get exercise, and are seen by a qualified vet if ill.

12. Potbellied pigs can be territorial if they feel threatened. They are naturally suspicious and cautious. They are emotional, at times, and need to feel safe and loved. They will not bite, unless provoked, just as other animals might do.

13. Potbellied pigs can be kept indoors or out. Pet pillows and blankets work well indoors. A dog house or shed, filled with hay and straw, provides secure outside quarters. They must be kept warm and protected from the elements if outside. They must be provided ample space to roam and explore.

14. Potbellied pigs need environments that are piggy proofed so they are always safe. They will try to eat anything, including wires, plants, gum, and cleaning supplies. If they don't receive attention and affection, they can become bored, unhappy, even aggressive and destructive.

15. Potbellied pigs may be considered farm animals and not allowed in certain neighborhoods, or cities. Be sure to check before bringing one home.

16. Potbellied pigs are very loyal to their families and may become very attached immediately.

17. Potbellied pigs do bond with other household pets, though it is probably a good idea to separate pigs and dogs.

*It is hard to find any other pet as adorable as these cute butterballs. However, they do grow up quickly, so it is always a good idea to interact with full grown potbellied pigs before deciding to get one.

*There is not a better companion than a potbellied pig, but only for the right owner. Human touch and interaction are as essential as a good diet for their emotional well-being.

*They are mostly non-allergenic, don't have fleas or rabies, and don't bark. You have to earn their trust and respect, rather like a cat.

*Perhaps the best idea is to adopt a potbellied pig from a sanctuary, pig rescue, or another organization both public and private. The following are only a few that can help you to decide if this is a good pet for your family: Ironwood Pig Sanctuary, Ross Mill Farm, Pigs Peace Sanctuary, North American Potbellied Pig Association, Best Friends Animal Sanctuary, Happy Trails Farm Animal Sanctuary, Pigasus Homestead, Hamalot Potbellied Pig Rescue, Lil'Orphan Hammies, Rooterville, www.pigplacementnetwork.com, and www.petpigs.com.

Thank you to the Ironwood Pig Sanctuary who are "dedicated to eliminating the suffering of pot-bellied pigs by promoting spaying and neutering, assisting owners and other sanctuaries, and promoting a permanent home in a safe nurturing environment for those that are abandoned, abused, neglected, or unwanted."

The Williams Family Shares a Rat 'Tail'

Being kind to a difference of opinion whether it involves a tail or not

Story by Jennifer Foreman de Grassi Williams

Watercolors by Bobbi Kelly

Dedicated to all those parents that said "Yes"
to their children who wanted to have a pet rat,
and to all those millions of rats who never got
an opportunity to be loved, who lived their lives
in labs being prodded and poked, sacrificing
their lives and undergoing painful and invasive
procedures. I pray there is a rat heaven.

And of course, this book is dedicated to Cheeky
Monkey, Baby So, and Peanut, my beautiful
granddaughters.

Thank you, once again, to Dr. Alicia Konsella
DVM, for her sage knowledge about all things
great and small.

Story number 7 is about pet rats. Just hearing the word rat makes some people's skin crawl, while other people defend their little spirits as the best rodent a person could love. As a young girl, nobody I knew had a rat as a pet. As a matter of fact, our parents told us that rats were big, ugly, scary, and diseased creatures that gave us bad dreams. Part of what they said was true. Large sewer rats were all our parents knew. I'm not certain just when we decided rats would make great domestic pets. Perhaps lab technicians, who used them in a plethora of experiments, found that

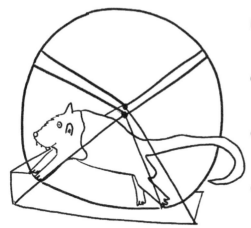 many of their lab specimens had

actually shown a sensitive, caring,

and loyal nature. My family,

as one of many, is overjoyed

that rats are being offered for

companions. One idea, that most people will agree,

is that a rat's tail is not a particularly lovely sight. If

rats came without tails, I am certain more people

would have them, and not shriek when they see it

attached to such a soft and cuddly being. Rats have

just the right combination of play and snuggles. Like

visits from my own Mother when she stayed

in our household of pets, we'd do everything to shelter her from having to experience a rat tail. Ideas to tape, paint, or cover the tail with clothing or bows were all considerations. There is no doubt

we have completely discounted that rats experience pain and fear, shown by the fact that we still count on them as specimens in a lab. You've only to have a pet rat to know that finding another non-living option to use in all kinds of experiments would be the kind and ethical thing to do. This story is about the joy my family found in this 'unsung hero' of pets. Perhaps, and after reading our story, a family who would have never considered having a rat, might just look at them as something other than snake food. And that 'tail' my Mother never liked, might be no stranger than that piece of hair many humans sport, hanging in a strange strand down the back of a human head.

The kids had waited weeks and weeks to hear those very words,

That Grandma would be here in days and they knew what that meant;

Their sweet pet rat with his long tail would have to find a way,

To hide from her his great long tail in a dress or giant tent.

Sweet Zeekie had a gray-black head and fur so long and soft,

Truth be known his hairless tail was really cute and round;

And he was such a happy guy and loved to eat all food,

That he got big and his poor feet couldn't even touch the ground.

There is a great big lesson, for
each of us to know,

That if you treat with kindness,
then in turn you'll get it too;

Rats just love attention and they
won't attack and bite,

Unless they think your finger is
some food to gnaw and chew.

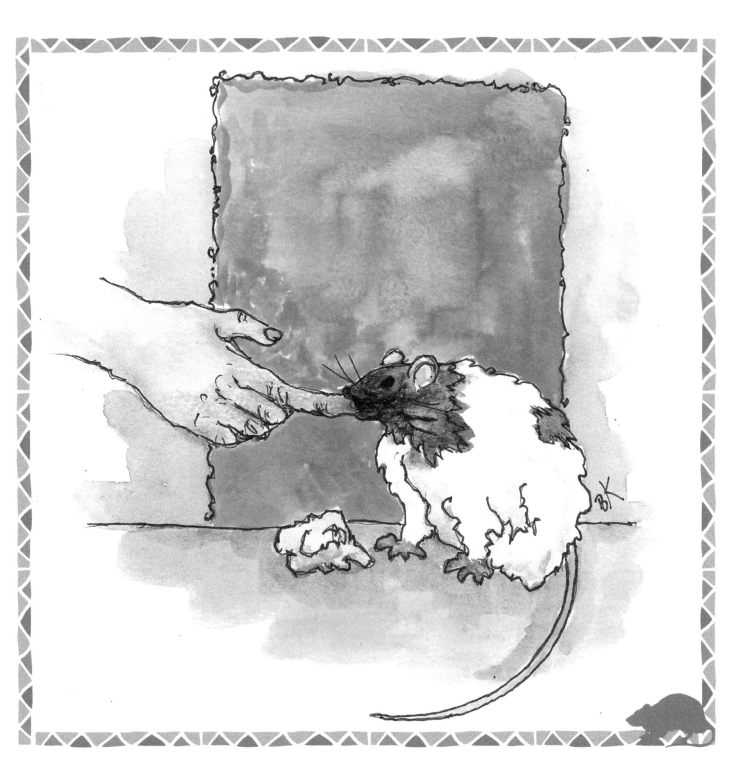

When Zeek smelled cake or pizza
next to his big bowl of food,

You'd see him crawl onto the
table not knowing where to start;

The frosting was so sweet and
yummy, but the pizza was the best,

And certainly not very good for
his big tender heart.

Baby Zeek had many toys ~ a ball and wind-up box,

He'd pull the rope so very hard to make his wagon shake;

And then the doll inside the box would jump up very high,

But Zeekie wasn't fond at all of the big, and green old snake.

Funny Zeek would jump up high
onto the big bathtub,

He loved to lick the bubbles and
watch as Duckie floats;

But oh he was so careful not to
fall in with the girls,

While listening to them laugh and
smile, and tell their silly jokes.

Zeekie was so friendly and loved so very much,

And how he liked to wander when he came outside his cage;

And boy he'd like to run and hide or play with everyone,

Cuz' being kind to your pet rat is good at any age.

Fifi was another rat and Fifle was one too,

Along with kind old Zeekie there was love inside the house;

The girls would sneak their furry friends into their beds at night,

And even though these friends were rats, they were quiet as a mouse.

Fifi was the sweetest mom and
Fifle the best dad,

With seven little 'kittens' running
here and there to boot;

And anyone who saw them and
the way they loved their kids,

Would say that rats are just the
best and that their tails are cute.

It is a fact that rats are smart and figure out so much,

I bet that if they had a chance they'd try to read a book;

Perhaps the story Stuart Little or maybe Charlotte's Web,

And follow Templeton the rat on the journey's that he took.

A lick, a nibble, or a whisper in
your ear will say,

My love for you will grow and grow
as big as any whale;

I know that you may have to gulp
and look the other way,

If, though you think I'm pretty
special, you just don't like my tail.

The End

Pet Rat Facts:

1. Pet rats are one of the friendliest rodents for children to have as pets, because they are very affectionate and responsive to being handled.

2. Pet rats love to explore their environments, and are very happy to be out of their cage for extended periods of time. However, they do love to chew on a variety of things so must be monitored.

3. Pet rats are very social and do very well in pairs, especially if they were litter mates.

4. Pet rats are called Does if female, and Bucks if male. Baby rats are called Kittens, Pups, or Pinkies.

5. Pet rats are not usually compatible with other family pets, or other types of rodents, unless closely monitored.

6. Pet rats develop a hierarchy of dominance as they get older, and the Bucks may begin to act out against each other. Introduction of rats to each other should be done carefully and patiently, especially the older they are.

7. Pet rats have a life span of only about two years.

8. Pet rats can weigh over a pound if male, and over a half pound if female. If they have been fed a poor diet, or too much food, they might get so big that their back legs walk on the fat of their sides! Obesity can be a serious health problem and shorten the life of your rat.

9. Pet rats require a large cage that provides a healthy, safe, and comfortable home.

10. Pet rats thrive in a cage that is cleaned at least once a week, as they are fastidious pets that continually groom themselves.

11. Pet rats require clean bedding material, like shredded paper or untreated wood shavings.

12. Pet rats will eat just about anything that is offered to them. However, they should be given a rat specific diet sold at pet stores. They love table scraps, fruits, vegetables, and supplements of fat and protein, especially when young.

13. Pet rats need a permanent source of water. A pet water bottle should be provided inside the cage at all times. They might even let you know when it is empty.

14. Pet rats will breed indiscriminately if Bucks and Does are left together. Separating the Doe and Buck after mating is very important, as Does can get

pregnant immediately after giving birth. Unless you are prepared to find homes for the Kittens, leave only same sex pairs together.

15. Pet rats are born after about three weeks, and there can be as many as ten Kittens. Wean Kittens after about five weeks and separate into same sex groups.

16. Pet rats are susceptible to a variety of health issues, including skin dryness and scabs, respiratory problems, weight gain or loss, and benign or cancerous tumors.

17. Pet rats do not need vaccinations, but should see a veterinarian if they are acting lethargic, not eating, have tumors, or seem out of sorts.

*Pet rats are instinctively scavengers and will grab food if given the opportunity. Sometimes fingers that smell like food might be mistaken for it.

*Pet rats, like ferrets, collect little trinkets that they may hide, or shred as part of their environment.

*Pet rats may play with small toys, like bells, balls, feathers, etc.

*Pets rats are instinctive hunters. While not a problem if monitored, never leave a rat with smaller pets like mice, lizards, hermit crabs, etc.

*Pet rats are very tame by nature, but their normal instinct to run away and hide, or even bite if afraid or provoked, is normal.

*Pet rats have not been bred to live in the wild, so never release them into it.

*Pet rats love to groom. Grooming can take on a variety of meanings. Mothers will groom their babies as part of their care. Young rats may groom each other as an act of socialization. Forced grooming can happen by dominant males. And sometimes, your pet rat might lick your hand, arm, toes, or cheeks because you taste good, or because they consider you a part of their family.

*Pet rats usually figure out their own pecking order, and aren't usually mean. Occasionally, a rat that has been abused, neglected, or hormonal might show some aggressive behavior. Sometimes, this behavior is learned or passed down. Aggressive male rats can be neutered. Veterinarians recommend spaying females, too, to reduce their risk for tumors. Rats, like cats, need to trust to

Do you know that rats LAUGH?

be good pets. Depending on their prior experiences, this may be challenging.

*Pregnant rats, or those with babies, may act protective. They should be placed in a cage by themselves, and with their babies. Sometimes pet rat mothers will eat their sick or stillborn young. It is nature's way to keep the environment clean, and not to attract predators.

*Pet rats grind their teeth, called bruxing, and do it when the pet is content or stressed. It is also a way to wear down their teeth.

*Pet rats are very intelligent and can get bored. Providing them with small wooden toys, and paper to shred for their beds, is a good idea.

*Pet rats, especially males, may leave a urine trail of drops to mark their territories. As they are not litter-trained, they will leave pellets behind as they go.

*Pet rats display a variety of behaviors according to how they have been raised. People who interact with their rats and take time to observe them, usually can read their rats better than people who have not spent much time with their pets. How an owner communicates with their rat can definitely affect their behavior.

*Pet rats should never be punished, but treated gently and kindly. They will learn to trust and be gentle and kind in return.

The Author

Jennifer Foreman de Grassi Williams

Jennifer was born and raised in Oakland, California, but came to Idaho in 1972 as the wife of an Air Force pilot. She began her teaching career at Mountain Home High School where she taught art for 25 years before teaching art at Skyview High School in Nampa. She earned her BFA in Art Education from Mississippi State University and her Master's degree in Art from Boise State University.

Jennifer lives in Idaho with her husband, Kirk (who still shoots his age in golf), where she has been an art educator for 44 years. Jennifer has been an adjunct professor at Boise State University, George Fox University and the College of Idaho. Jennifer has received numerous state and national awards in her teaching career, including the Governor's Award in

Art Education, US West Teacher of the Year, Boise State's Distinguished Alumni Award and Women Making History Award, ING's 1st Place National Unsung Heroes Award, the National Education Association's Teaching Excellence Award, Idaho's Art Teacher of the Year and was the 2002 Idaho Teacher of the Year. In 2016, Jennifer was one of only five teachers, nationwide, inducted into the NATIONAL TEACHERS HALL OF FAME in Emporia, Kansas, and is the first Idaho teacher to have ever been recognized by the President of the United States for this award. Jennifer is a published artist, having written two art textbooks and many articles. This is volume 1 of a hardback book that includes seven stories, previously published as softcover individual books. These mostly factual stories are about the plethora of sentient beings that always seem to find their way into her life. Jennifer passionately advocates for all creatures.

Jennifer has taken art to tiny one room school houses for over 40 years with her 'Project Van Go'. Two years ago she celebrated this milestone at the little red school house on the prairie in Prairie, Idaho. Her greatest work, she says, is that of 'WA' to her precious granddaughters, and Mother to four amazing children: Hillary an Investigator for Human Resources living in the warmth of Arizona, Tyler (Lauren) a Doctor of Physical Therapy residing in the Bay Area and exploring all things that test any limit, Jessica (Kyle) a high school Science teacher in Idaho and amazing mother to our precious 'cheeky monkey' Norah, Harper 'peanut', and Emily (Jason) who is a School Counselor and stay at home Mommy to darling Sonja Hope. In her free time, Jennifer rehabilitates wild and domesticated animals. At every opportunity she volunteers at the Makauwahi Cave Reserve on Kaua'i where her two giant sulcata tortoises, Shelly and Lily, are part of a project that promotes the propagation of native Hawaiian plants. Jennifer donates profits from her books to many organizations. Her greatest inspiration was her Mother who passed away 5 years ago. Jennifer smiles at the journey that is her life since she was Miss San Francisco Cable Car 1968.

The Watercolorist

Bobbi Kelly

Bobbi Kelly taught high school
art in Mountain Home for many
years before retiring and moving to
Moscow, Idaho, where she resides
with her daughter, Sandra, and their devoted dog, Holly.
She is an active member of the Idaho Watercolor Society
and the Palouse Watercolor Society, and teaches adult
painting classes as well as doing volunteer art projects
with elementary students. Bobbi enjoys painting local
and regional scenes of interest, in a style she thinks of as
"casual realism". "Illustrating Jennifer's children's books
is definitely a change of pace from my usual watercolor
subject matter," Bobbi says, "but one which is both
creatively demanding and delightful." Bobbi and Jennifer
have remained best friends for over four decades.
Examples of her work can be viewed on the Palouse
Watercolor Society website:
www.palousewatercolorsocius.com

Books by Jennifer Foreman de Grassi Williams can also be purchased individually:

The Williams Family Adopts Tiki Turtle

The Williams Family and a Very Beloved Dolly

The Williams Family Bids Aloha to Shell and Lily

The Williams Family and Andy Cat

The Williams Family and a Curious Stinky Minky

The Williams Family Rescues a Piggy Named Otis

The Williams Family Shares a Rat "Tail"

Introduction to Batik and Other Resists

Art 2 - Pottery, Sculpture, Batik and 3-D Design

For more information go to http://projectvango.org

* Located in each story is a small drawing of a pig. Did you find it?